REAL WORLD ECONOMICS™

How Trade Deficits Work

Kate Canino

ROSEN
PUBLISHING®

New York

*To my brother Joel Canino, who ever since he opened his first lemonade stand
has inspired me to always be aware of my finances*

Published in 2011 by The Rosen Publishing Group, Inc.
29 East 21st Street, New York, NY 10010

First Edition

Library of Congress Cataloging-in-Publication Data

Canino, Kate.
How trade deficits work / Kate Canino.
    p. cm.—(Real world economics)
Includes bibliographical references and index.
ISBN 978-1-4488-1271-4 (library binding)
1. Balance of trade—Juvenile literature. 2. International trade—Juvenile
literature. I. Title.
HF1014.C27 2011
382'.17—dc22

                                                                2010014527

Manufactured in the United States of America

CPSIA Compliance Information: Batch #W11YA: For further information, contact Rosen Publishing, New York, New York, at
1-800-237-9932.

On the cover: Freight containers headed to and from China occupy
a shipyard.

Contents

INTRODUCTION

Trade is the buying and selling of goods and services between countries. Goods include cars, cell phones, computers, and clothes. Tourism (traveling for pleasure) to other countries and banking are examples of traded services. Think about it this way: if a person takes an article of clothing from his or her closet and thinks about all of the people whose work went into that one piece of clothing, there will be many faces. First, you have a fashion designer that comes up with the idea for the shirt. That idea is sent to a company where someone approves it. The material to make the clothing is produced by a textile manufacturer. Then someone ships that material to a factory, where someone else makes the shirt. That same shirt is then packaged and shipped to a retail store. The retailer has an employee who takes it out of its packaging and puts it on the shelf. The consumer walks in and buys the shirt from an employee, and then the consumer takes it home. All of the people behind the product need to

get paid from the money that the consumer purchased that article of clothing for.

This goes for not just clothing, but for any type of goods and services that the average person consumes. All of these production phases may take place in a different country and still end up in your closet. The reason for the trade deficit in America is because we are purchasing more goods and services from outside of our country.

When the Berlin Wall fell in 1989, much of the world began to embrace the economic system of capitalism. As a result, businesses had even bigger markets of consumers, or buyers. Products such as American clothing, fast-food restaurants, and music quickly became popular all over the world. In the early 1990s, American companies sold millions of dollars in exports. But, according to John Stamos of Defender Capital, an investment firm in Charlotte, North Carolina, "We were at the same time overspending, so our imports surged."

The Berlin Wall fell in November 1989. This signified the breakdown of the German Communist system, which had dominated Eastern Europe for most of the twentieth century. The fall led to a capitalistic system, which opened wide the doors of trade.

Countries often report their trade balances. A trade balance is exports minus imports. A favorable trade balance is also called a trade surplus. This means that countries are selling more products to other countries than they are buying from them.

An unfavorable trade balance is called a trade deficit. Trade deficits happen when a country buys more products from other countries than it sells to them. Trade agreements, which set the rules for how countries buy and sell products from each other, affect trade balances. The North American Free Trade Agreement (NAFTA) and the World Trade Organization (WTO) were put in place to help more goods and services flow between countries by eliminating trade barriers. However, as will later be discussed, these agreements came with their own set of challenges, which affected America's trade balance.

The United States is currently running a trade deficit, but there are ways to change this. Both the government and the American people can make choices that can help reduce the trade deficit. Lowering the trade deficit is important because it affects job opportunities, standards of living, and the prices of goods and services.

CHAPTER ONE

THE TRADE DEFICIT UP CLOSE

When the term "trade deficit" is mentioned, whether it be on the news, in the classroom, or at the dinner table, people should pay attention because it is an economic phenomenon that affects everyone. It can affect the prices of goods and services that people buy or will want to purchase in the future. As a culture, we thrive on consuming products such as clothes, shoes, and electronics at low prices. That is why big-box stores such as Walmart and Target are so popular. They are large retail stores that buy goods in large quantities and can therefore offer lower prices for their products. So what does all of this have to do with the trade deficit? First, let's take a look at what is in the average American's wardrobe.

Grab anywhere from ten to fifteen items of clothing from the closet and then grab a world map or pull one up on the computer. Check the tags of each of article of clothing chosen and mark on the map where that item was made. For the average person, most of the tags will mention a country in Asia, such as China. Little of the clothing, if any, will have been

The reason why big-box stores such as Walmart can roll back, or reduce, their prices is because of the amount of products and services they purchase at low prices from foreign countries.

made in America. Do this also with shoes, toys, cell phones, and electronics, and the results may be very similar. If clothes and other products are not made in America, workers in a foreign country are getting paid to make them. So Americans

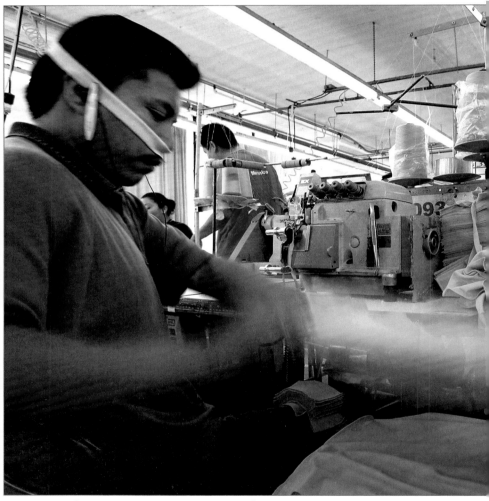

Foreign factories are paid less to manufacture goods for the United States. These factories are run like huge assembly lines that work hard to keep up with consumer demand.

are not getting paid to produce goods and services made in other countries.

Sometimes American products cost more than similar products made in foreign countries. Since people's demand for

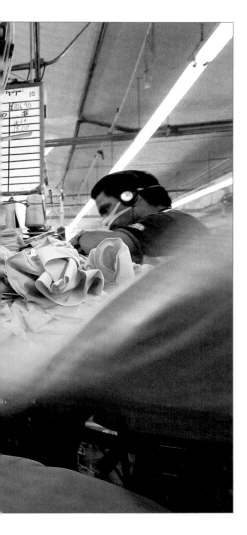

items depends mainly on price, this can lead people to buy more goods from foreign countries, or imports. If you walk into a local store that sells American-made clothes, notice how much more expensive the clothes are. Since consumers in America have gotten used to inexpensive prices, we keep importing more and more from Asia and exporting less, thus creating a trade imbalance, or a trade deficit.

Big-Box Versus Local Stores

Decades ago, the job scene looked very different than it does today. Many American workers worked in factories and were paid minimum wage. They might have received raises or benefits, such as health care and a retirement plan. Often, if a person worked in a factory, his or her child would be able to have a job in that same factory.

11

But today, with globalization, some American companies are choosing to send their factories abroad, where foreign workers, rather than Americans, are getting the jobs.

One reason that companies set up businesses in other countries is to lower their costs. For example, labor costs (the cost for companies to pay their workers) are a big part of the total cost of many products. Companies want to keep their total costs low because they can make more money. How much an item costs to produce also affects the item's price. If a company has lower costs, it can pass this along to the consumer in the form of lower prices. This makes consumers buy more products. It also allows companies to make more money.

One way that globalization has allowed companies to lower their costs is by allowing for lower labor costs. The average cost of paying a Chinese worker is $.50 an hour, as opposed to paying an American worker $7.25 for the same type of work (which is the minimum wage according to the U.S. Department of Labor). Hence, the retailer makes a larger profit on imports from China because it pays less for them. Retailers mark up the price of their products. This means that they charge more for an item than it costs for them to buy it. If a product costs less to make abroad and import, stores can charge higher

Textile manufacturers ship material to countries such as China, where products are made at a lower cost than in the United States. However, the quality often suffers because of the quick turnaround.

markups, make more money, and still offer competitive prices. The bottom line is that lower expenses mean more profits. And more and more, stores and consumers are finding lower costs abroad in the form of imports. More imports (combined with fewer exports) cause a trade deficit.

A retailer such as Target can import products from China and then mark them up and make 60 to 70 percent more than what they paid for them. However, if those same products were made in the United States, the retailer would have to pay more for them and then could only make 20 percent more because the retailer would have to buy those same products at a higher price.

For instance, if a person were to purchase a simple cotton T-shirt that has been made in a U.S. factory by American employees, it might cost about $20. This may be more expensive than a similar product imported from another country. But by purchasing this shirt, consumers are supporting both a U.S. retailer and American workers, and they are keeping money flowing through the U.S. economy. Purchasing goods and services made in the United States, rather than imported products, can also help improve the trade deficit.

What about the retailer's side? If it costs the store $12 to buy the shirt from the U.S. factory, the retailer may choose a markup of $12 per shirt to make $8 for every shirt it sells. If the retailer is paying more to stock American-made goods, it may also have fewer shirts on its shelves than if it imported them. Fewer shirts can mean less profit.

For example, if a retailer makes $8 on every shirt but only has ten of these shirts to sell, it earns an overall profit of $80. But if that same retailer had twenty shirts to sell, it would have earned $160 in profit.

Now take that same simple cotton T-shirt that has been made in a Chinese clothing factory by Chinese employees and then imported to the United States. The cost for the consumer to buy the shirt may be less—a lot less. Even if the price of the shirt is $12, the retailer can still make more money on each shirt because it costs so much less to buy each shirt. If the retailer paid $0.02 per imported shirt and sold each shirt to consumers for $12, the retailer makes $11.98 per shirt. That is significantly more than what the retailer made from selling American-made shirts. The retailer can also afford to put more shirts on the shelves, thus increasing inventory.

More shirts can mean more sales and more profits. For example, instead of purchasing ten shirts, the retailer could purchase thirty and make an overall profit of $359.40. That is $279.40 more than before. Multiply that number by the amount of stores that a retailer may have, and the profits are even greater. Also remember that price is related to the quantity demanded of a good. Because the shirts imported from China cost so much less, the retailer could offer a lower price. Consumers who are trying to save money or get the best deals are more likely to buy the less expensive cotton shirt. But both American and Chinese companies share the money that was made from the sale of the shirt.

DOMESTIC VERSUS FOREIGN LABOR

When people buy imports instead of similar goods that were made at home, the domestic companies that make these similar products suffer. Their sales decrease, which leads to layoffs because they do not need as many employees. If a store's sales severely decrease, it may be even forced to close, which means more job losses. Lost jobs also mean a loss of income for the fired employees. This leads to less money flowing into the economy.

Walmart by the Numbers

- Every week, 100 million people shop at Walmart's 3,400 American stores.
- There are 1.2 million Walmart employees in the United States and internationally,
- Walmart hires six hundred thousand new employees each year, and the company's turnover rate is 44 percent, which is close to the retail industry average.
- Walmart's sales first topped $1 billion in 1979.
- There are thirty-five Walmart Supercenters in China.
- Walmart estimates that it imports $15 billion worth of Chinese products each year; others suggest the number may be even higher.
- Walmart accounts for 8 percent of total U.S. retail sales, excluding automobiles.
- The average full-time hourly wage for a Walmart employee is $9.98. The average full-time hourly wage in metro areas (defined as areas with a population of fifty thousand or more) is $10.38. In some urban areas, it is higher: $11.03 in Chicago, Illinois; $11.08 in San Francisco, California; and $11.20 in Austin, Texas.

If people spend less on goods and services, more companies have to cut back on spending, lay off workers, and possibly close. This is known as an economic downturn. Buying more imported goods worsens the trade deficit and affects a country's economic performance.

Due to the examples stated above, big-box stores can gain substantial market share because they can sell very similar products for half the price. This can put small local stores out of business because it is impossible for them to compete. Big-box stores also buy products in greater quantity or bulk, which costs them less in the long run. This is known as economies of scale: as companies buy more of a product, each additional item costs less. To stay competitive, many big-box stores send out plants and factories to other countries, where labor costs are significantly less. This adds to the trade deficit because then we have to import those products and we are making less here in the United States.

CHAPTER TWO

SOME CAUSES OF THE AMERICAN TRADE DEFICIT

For every event or economic phenomenon that occurs, there are causes and effects. This holds true for the trade deficit in the United States. It is not just the fact that retailers have sent their factories to foreign countries and are then bringing the goods into the country as imports. There are many different causes for the U.S. trade deficit.

GLOBALIZATION

Globalization is when there is an increased flow of goods, services, money, and ideas from beyond national borders. Multinational corporations drive globalization. They can move their businesses to other countries where labor and materials are less expensive. The downside to this is that it eliminates jobs in the United States. Also, because labor laws are different in other countries, workers in countries such as China, Taiwan, and Indonesia may have few or no rights when it comes to their job environment. There are also lower environmental standards and wages for workers, which is why it's important to be mindful of where products are made. Two major events that changed the way that the United States trades with other countries are the signing of NAFTA and the creation of the WTO. Both of these events caused a surge in imports and exports that resulted in the trade deficit that we are dealing with today.

NAFTA

On December 8, 1993, President Bill Clinton signed NAFTA into law. It took effect on January 1, 1994. This opened up trade with Canada and Mexico. It created one of the world's largest zones of free trade with the hope of more economic growth for Canada, Mexico, and the United States. NAFTA set the rules for trade and investment between the three countries by eliminating many tariff and nontariff barriers. Tariffs are taxes placed on imported goods. They make foreign goods more expensive, which makes consumers want to buy less of them. Tariffs also provide revenue for the government, since the government receives the tax money. Nontariff barriers also try to limit trade between countries. A quota is an example of a nontariff barrier. It limits the amount of a foreign good that can be brought into a country. Trade agreements such as NAFTA reduce these barriers and increase trade between countries.

NAFTA also strove to increase economic growth and competition among companies. This would benefit families, workers, manufacturers, farmers, and consumers because companies

On September 14, 1993, President Bill Clinton signed the North American Free Trade Agreement. Its main goal was to reduce the barriers of trade and create broader international cooperation.

now worked to increase the quality of their products. During this period, the strength of the U.S. economy led the country to increase imports. The United States had more money to spend, so the demand for goods and services increased.

The positive side of creating a free trade environment with Mexico and Canada not only included more money in American pockets, but also more competition and the expansion of American business. The negative side was that the United States saw how much less expensive it was to place its businesses in Mexico. It could pay foreign workers less than American workers to produce the same products. At first, this might seem positive, but it meant that many Americans would lose their jobs to foreign workers. According to I. M. Destler, author of *American Trade Politics*, the prospect of NAFTA "alarmed organized labor and some environmental groups." Organized labor groups felt threatened by open trade with a "low wage" neighbor because the United States was already losing its jobs to foreign competition.

THE WORLD TRADE ORGANIZATION

Not only was America importing more from Mexico, but China also began expanding its economic ties or relations with the West. In the 1990s, China entered the WTO. The WTO was constructed to lower trade barriers and encourage multilateral trade, or trade between many countries at one time. It is the only global international organization dealing with the rules of trade between nations. The goal is to help producers of goods and services, exporters, and importers conduct their business. Also, by lowering trade barriers among countries, it promotes interdependence and breaks down the barriers between peoples and nations.

With all of the international capital flow from free trade, the U.S. dollar kept on getting stronger. This made imports more attractive because Americans could get a better deal on consumer products and services. It also made the prices of U.S. exports less competitive. For instance, it costs more to make products such as cell phones in the United States than China, so we end up importing more products than we export because of cost. Therefore, more countries invest in the United

States because Americans purchase so much. This creates unequal relationships with U.S. trading partners because U.S. markets are more open to importing goods and services than any other country. Since the United States imports so much,

The World Trade Organization is a place where nations go to discuss any trade issues they may face.

it gives more power to the countries that we are trading with in terms of prices and restrictions. For instance, if a person is used to paying $89 for a pair of Nike shoes that are manufactured in Asia and that is the only place that makes them, the

Because the United States consumes so many imports at such low prices, Americans have become dependent on international products and trade.

Asian market can raise the prices of Nike shoes as much as it sees fit. This is because America no longer makes Nikes on its own soil, and countries in Asia know there is a great demand for the shoe and that the U.S. consumer will pay a higher amount.

The WTO helps prevent occurrences such as dumping, which is considered a predatory practice that increases imports. Manufacturers do this to increase sales. An example would be when a manufacturer exports a product at a price that is below the price it charges in its own country or below what it costs to make the product. This increases the manufacturer's sales because lower prices mean that more people will buy the product.

Antidumping laws have been put into effect to stop this from happening because it is considered an unfair trade practice, as it may cause material injury to the importing markets. Dumping affects the trade deficit because it causes the United States to import more than it exports.

NAFTA Statistics

- **NAFTA created the world's largest free trade area, which links 444 million people producing $17 trillion worth of goods and services.**
- **Trade between the United States and its NAFTA partners has soared since the agreement took effect. U.S. trade with NAFTA members totaled $1 trillion in 2007.**
- **The United States traded $967 billion in total goods with NAFTA countries Canada and Mexico during 2008.**
- **The U.S. goods and services trade deficit with NAFTA members was $116 billion in 2007.**
- **Canada and Mexico were the top two purchasers of U.S. exports in 2008. (Canada imported $261.2 billion in U.S. goods, and Mexico imported $151.2 billion.)**
- **Canada was the largest importer of goods to the United States in 2008, totaling $339.5 billion. Mexico was the third largest supplier of imported goods to the United States, with a total of $125.9 billion.**

NAFTA AND THE WTO

NAFTA, along with the WTO, has created more opportunities for trade and fostered interdependence throughout the world. It has increased competition and forced nations to improve technology and efficiency when producing goods and services so that they can remain competitive. It has also inspired innovative thinking and the creation of new businesses.

However, because of imbalances such as higher oil prices in the United States, NAFTA and the WTO have also opened the door to less expensive foreign goods and services, which have increased imports and the U.S. trade deficit. They have also encouraged companies to remain competitive, even at the cost of shipping jobs abroad and increasing the trade deficit.

MYTHS and FACTS

MYTH The U.S. trade deficit is caused by unfair trade practices abroad.

FACT The U.S. trade deficit is a reflection of the flow of capital (money) across the borders of foreign countries and the amount that America is importing versus exporting.

MYTH The trade deficit is a sign of economic weakness.

FACT Americans' standard of living has increased because they can afford to purchase more goods than their trading partners in foreign countries. This is seen as a sign of strength.

MYTH NAFTA has resulted in job losses.

FACT Since NAFTA was put into place in 1994, total employment has grown by almost forty million jobs.

CHAPTER THREE
TRADE DEFICITS TAKING SHAPE

With any economic phenomenon, there are different causes. With those causes come effects. America's trade deficit has provided many benefits as trade became easier. The U.S. trade deficit grew rapidly as trade between other countries became easier with NAFTA and the WTO in place. Free trade with other countries quickly led to increased U.S. competitiveness in the global marketplace. It also gave the United States a chance to share its products with the rest of the world, thus globalizing trade. This gave the United States access to goods and services that may not have otherwise been available to it. An example would be the fact that when walking into the international food section of an American grocery store, a person has the ability to purchase foods from all over the world.

This access to inexpensive products and services has increased the standard of living for Americans in such a way that they can buy more for their money. Americans are able to fill their homes and apartments with more goods such as food, clothing, housewares, and cars. They are also used to buying these products at lower prices. The majority of households shop at one-stop shopping establishments because they are more

Hot products such as the Apple iPad are often made overseas and contribute to America's dependence on international trade.

convenient. If people could only buy things that were made in the United States from locally owned stores, the prices of those goods and services would be much higher. This would mean that the standard of living would have to decrease because it

would become more difficult for people to afford the products and services they were used to. Once a person gets used to having these things, it is hard for that person to change. Our society tells us that we need to keep up with the latest trends, be it clothes, cell phones, and iPods or the decor in our rooms.

The average Walmart carries approximately 150,000 products. There is no way a local business that only carries American-made products could possibly compete.

Since it is so easy to buy all of this stuff, it has influenced the way we shop and the way we live. It becomes clear how the trade deficit has had such a tremendous influence on our daily lives when a person thinks about all of the material items and services that he or she receives every day. When getting ready for school, a person gets dressed. Most of the clothes that a teenager owns are not made in the United States. The average American teenager wants to keep up with the latest fashions, from clothes to electronic accessories such as cell phones, iPods, and cameras.

Some people feel that by shopping at a local farmer's market, they not only support the domestic economy but also get to know the seller of the products purchased.

In order to afford these things, the average American teenager, or his or her parents, shops wherever there is the best deal. These deals are usually at big-box stores. Unless parents are shopping at their local farmer's markets, the majority of the food

on the kitchen table is not from the United States. The gas that goes into the vehicle that takes a teenager to school is not from the United States; it is imported. Within a school, whether it be school supplies, the clocks on the wall, or the textbooks that are required, these products are mainly imported. After-school activities are also influenced by the trade deficit. Check the labels on sports equipment to see where it is from. The typical American teenager is surrounded by foreign imports and marketing tools to get him or her to buy more stuff.

TRADE DEFICIT TAKES ROOT

A trade deficit takes root when consumers get used to acquiring goods and services at a lower cost. Americans become dependent on the lower prices and easy access to these good and services.

Argument for Shopping at a Farmer's Market

- **More money is spent locally, keeping money in the pockets of American farmers.**
- **Reinforces local jobs and maintains local employment.**
- **Reduces dependency on food imported internationally and increases reliance on local food.**
- **Reduces dependency on foreign oil because the food travels a shorter distance.**
- **Provides an outlet for local produce, helping start new local businesses and expand existing ones.**
- **Food has less packaging, which reduces the need for petroleum-based packaging.**

A deficit provides increased sales and employment in the international market. The current trade deficit for the United States, according to the U.S. Census, is as follows:

- The goods and services deficit was $380.7 billion in 2009, down from $695.9 billion in 2008.
- Exports decreased $273.5 billion to $1,553.1 billion in 2009. Goods were $1,045.6 billion, and services were $507.5 billion.
- Imports decreased $588.8 billion to $1,933.7 billion in 2009. Goods were $1,562.5 billion, and services were $371.2 billion.

- For goods, the deficit was $517.0 billion in 2009, down from $840.3 billion in 2008.
- For services, the surplus was $136.3 billion in 2009, down from $144.3 billion in 2008.

IMPACTS OF THE TRADE DEFICIT

The trade deficit has decreased, but America is still exporting less and importing more. The trade deficit continues to impact the United States when the cycle of exporting less and importing more costs American jobs. This can be seen in the unemployment rate, which jumped from 5.8 percent in 2008 to 10 percent in 2009. However, according to the U.S. Department of Labor, the unemployment rate fell from 10 percent to 9.7 percent in January 2010. "Employment fell in construction and in transportation and warehousing, while temporary help services and retail trade added jobs," reports the federal agency. So there has been a slight turnaround in unemployment rates because the United States is starting to realize that the economy could suffer further if things do not change.

The trade deficit also impacts interest rates on things such as credit cards, mortgage rates, and school loans because America owes money to other countries. These are all areas that will affect a young adult's life when he or she graduates high school, moves on to college, and buys his or her first home. The United States carries a lot of debt to other countries because it buys more than it can—so much so that countries such as China are lending money to the United States so that consumers can continue to buy cheap products. Americans have taken on a lot of debt, and there are not enough jobs to pay off that debt. Therefore, raising interest rates forces people to pay more for credit cards, loans, and mortgages. This has a tremendous impact on teenagers as they prepare to take out loans for college.

Credit cards make shopping easy for consumers. This can be dangerous, however, as the convenience makes it easy to rack up credit card debt.

Let's say that a loan for $10,000 is needed in order to attend the school of choice, but the interest rate on that loan is 10 percent every year. Every year the loan is not paid off, a person has to add 10 percent to that $10,000, or whatever amount is

left owing. When the economy is thriving and there is more cash flow among Americans, interest rates are lowered. When those rates are lowered, it is easier to pay off debt.

The trade deficit has had a major impact on the price of oil. Americans are dependent on oil for transportation and to make products such as crayons, dishwashing liquid, deodorant, eyeglasses, plastics, CDs, DVDs, tires, and even bubble gum. Economists expect that the gap between imports and exports will continue to grow if oil prices rise. According to a *New York Times* article from June 2009, "American demand for petroleum is relatively inelastic, so rising oil prices will tend to push up oil imports and the deficit. And recession aside, oil prices have trended upward for most of the past decade." The reason why the demand for oil is

Americans have a tremendous dependency on foreign oil. Because oil is a nonrenewable resource, Americans need to start thinking of ways to decrease their reliance on this valuable commodity.

inelastic or inflexible is because, as stated before, Americans are used to a certain lifestyle.

In all instances, the wallets of parents are directly influenced. With a high unemployment rate, rising cost of living, steeper oil prices, and increased interest rates, it is a struggle for most parents to keep up with the things that their teenagers feel they need. It is important to understand that if parents are struggling financially, it is better to help them figure out ways to reduce spending, as opposed to demanding more. This will not only decrease the amount of stress on parents, but it will also help decrease the impact of the trade deficit.

CHAPTER FOUR

THE GLOBAL EFFECTS

When free trade took root, it created jobs, increased people's incomes, and raised the standard of living. So when NAFTA was put in place, there were many benefits for all three countries involved. The same happened when China entered the WTO. All of a sudden, the United States, along with other countries, had more places to import and export products.

Picture the house a person lives in as a separate country from his or her neighbors. Around each house is a fence that does not allow a person to see what talents and skills are in the separate households. The talents and skills in one house are very different from those in another. The foods they eat, the clothes they buy, and the hobbies and skills they have acquired all look a little different. But because of the fence that is around each of their houses, no one is able to access and benefit from the talents and skills of their neighbors. There is not a strong sense of community or interdependence because of the barriers

Free trade has allowed the world to become more connected as countries become dependent on each other for goods and services. Complications arise when there is too much dependence on foreign trade or a country finds itself with a trade deficit.

the fences create. Let's say a person in the neighborhood was really good at landscaping. If the fence was not there, anyone could ask that landscaper to come over and give some tips and provide landscaping services. There would be a better sense of community within the neighborhood because other people would be able to benefit from the talents and skills of the landscaper. When NAFTA was put into place and China joined the WTO, the fences came down all of a sudden and the world was able to enjoy the talents, skills, and products that each individual country had to offer and was now able to share. Thus, a sense of community and interdependence between the countries resulted.

The U.S. trade deficit has had obvious repercussions on other countries because it continues to grow the more we import and export from other countries. The global effects are both positive and negative. This chapter will focus on Canada, Mexico, and China because they are the major countries that America exports to and imports from.

China and the United States

- **China and the United States have been trading partners since 1979.**
- **In 1979, the total value of the U.S.-to-China trade was $2.4 billion.**
- **By 2005, the total value of the U.S.-to-China trade was $211.6 billion.**
- **Today, the United States is China's largest trading partner and top export destination.**
- **In February 1985, Chinese imports to the United States began growing, and they continue to do so each year.**
- **In 2007, America's trade deficit with China exceeded $256 billion and grows about $1 billion each day.**
- **On December 11, 2001, China joined the World Trade Organization.**
- **In the United States, cheap imports from China have benefited American consumers by keeping product prices low.**
- **The U.S. trade deficit with China has grown to such an extent that many worry that the U.S. economy is too dependent on the flow of cheap goods.**

CANADA

Since NAFTA was enforced in January 1994, agricultural exports from Canada have nearly doubled. Some of Canada's exports to the United States consist of fresh fruits and vegetables, pet food, vegetable oils, soybean meal, eggs, juices, and processed fruits and vegetables. According to an article in the *Vancouver Sun*, "The volume of trade among the partners has tripled, economic growth has soared, businesses have become more competitive (and profitable), millions of jobs have been created, wages have increased, and governments have reaped the benefit of higher revenues." Canada also has more access to the Mexican market. Mexico is Canada's thirteenth largest export market and fourth largest import source.

According to the Foreign Affairs and International Trade Web site, because of NAFTA, Canadian business travelers have better access to the United States and Mexico. They can count on improved access to the United States and Mexico in order to seek out any business opportunities created by the agreement. Because the fences have come down, it is easier for countries like Canada to conduct business and remain competitive because the market of people is has contact with has dramatically increased.

However, Canada has its own trade deficit to deal with, just as the United States does. There are many benefits of free trade; however, this is the first time since 1976 that Canada has imported more goods than it has exported Also, because the United States is Canada's largest importer, Americans are spending less and the dollar is not worth as much. Therefore, Americans are not buying as much and Canadians are not making as much off of the United States. This adds to their current trade deficit because they are exporting less because demand has decreased. Douglas Porter, an economist for BMO Capital Markets, states that Canada has "feasted for decades on a backdrop of ravenous U.S. demand. With that appetite now on the strictest diet imaginable, our trade outlook has withered accordingly." This means that the United States has been buying goods from Canada at such a high rate and for so long that Canada has become dependent on the United States to keep its economy healthy. But now that the United States is in trouble, Canadians don't have as much money to spend. This has a negative effect on the Canadian economy.

MEXICO

When Mexico first joined NAFTA, its economic opportunities increased. The agreement eliminated tariffs, so Mexico's farm exports increased dramatically. Mexico is the top export destination for beef, rice, soybean meal, corn sweeteners, apples, and beans. It is also the second largest destination for corn, soybeans, and oils. However, NAFTA has also had negative consequences for the unemployment rate of these same Mexican farms that were once doing so well. Because the United States is also producing the same products at lower prices, this lowered the prices of the food that Mexico sells, which means that Mexican farmers are making less money. As a result of this, "millions of Mexican farm workers are now unemployed, and many have migrated to the United States," according to PBS.org.

There are many Mexicans in the United States who are working low-wage jobs as illegal immigrants. American companies

Many American companies hire illegal immigrants, putting the issue of immigration at the forefront of critical debate.

pay them less and offer them no benefits, as opposed to hiring an American citizen that would cost them more money. Because the United States has such a tremendous trade deficit, U.S. companies will pay as little as they can to produce goods. They then sell those goods for as much as they can in order to make an even larger profit.

CHINA

The influence that China has had on the U.S. trade deficit is tremendous. Countries like China are lending the United States money so that Americans can buy more of what they make. It is like when parents loan their teenaged son or daughter $50 to buy a much-desired pair of shoes. The teenager becomes obligated to pay back his or her parents. If the teenager only makes $10 a week in allowance, it will take five weeks for him or her to repay the loan. However, during those five weeks, other things come up that the teenager may want to spend money on, such as movies, clothes, or dinner at a restaurant. The more a teenager borrows from his or her parents, the more in debt the teenager becomes, thus creating an ever-more dependent financial relationship. The United States is dependent on China because of its debt. Parents may forgive the debt that their son or daughter has accumulated, but China will not forgive America's debt. This gives China power over America because that debt negatively influences the American economy.

China's major exports are office machines, data processing equipment, telecommunications equipment and other electrical machinery, and apparel. The average American owns a large

China's shipping containers line the West Coast as more and more products are brought over. America is currently so dependent on Chinese products that it would be detrimental to the U.S. economy if Americans were to stop purchasing Chinese imports.

portion of goods made from China because he or she can purchase them cheaper than the products made here. Americans
are not only dependent on China for loans but also for inexpensive products.

Another concern with China is that the government is
artificially keeping the value of its currency (the yuan) low
compared to the U.S. dollar. Doing so creates a large trade
imbalance between the two countries. It makes Chinese products sold in the United States cheaper and U.S. goods more
expensive in China. These types of practices add to the trade
deficit because America is selling fewer exports.

CHAPTER FIVE

THE TRADE DEFICIT TODAY

Because of the trade deficit's negative impact on the United States, the American government is starting to take action in order to get the country back on its feet, particularly when it comes to the amount it is exporting to other countries. There is a strong push to get small and medium-sized local businesses to export outside of the United States. The general public is also waking up to the fact that changes need to be made as budgets are getting tighter, interest rates are increasing, and the standard of living is getting higher.

THE NATIONAL EXPORT INITIATIVE

On January 27, 2010, President Barack Obama gave his State of the Union address. He discussed his plan to "rescue, rebuild, and restore America." This included the launch of the National Export Initiative. He stated that he wants to see U.S. exports double over the next five years, which will create two million

President Barack Obama, in his State of the Union address, introduced the National Export Initiative, which has been put into place to help reduce the American trade deficit.

new jobs in America. The more products that are made in this country, the more jobs that will be supported here.

Obama said the National Export Initiative will "help farmers and small businesses increase their exports and reform

export controls consistent with national security." This will greatly influence the future of young adults because the more jobs created now, the more jobs there will be when they graduate from high school and college. Within the next five years, those reading this book will be on the search for employment. If this initiative is successful, the jobs will be there. More jobs for Americans means more money filling the pockets of Americans.

According to Secretary of Commerce Gary Locke, the National Export Initiative is going to "sharpen the government's focus on the barriers that prevent U.S. companies from getting free and fair access to foreign markets." The Office of the U.S. Trade Representative is working to provide exporters with new market access opportunities by opening markets in key growth areas such as Asia. It will do this through the Trans Pacific Partnership (TPP), which is an agreement that could set a new standard for trade agreements with strong labor, environmental, and market admission standards. Locke states, "The United States is the most open major economy in the world. And that's not going to change!"

This push to increase the United States' exports is part of an ongoing focus to keep America competitive in the global market. When trading with many different countries, there is always the risk that not everyone will follow the rules. Global free trade only works when there is a system of rules that every party follows. Many Americans hope that the National Export Initiative will encourage countries to honor their agreements, thus creating a stronger interdependence among nations.

SMALL AND MEDIUM BUSINESSES

There is currently a strong drive in America to start reversing the trade deficit, especially since the National Export Initiative. The positive side of a trade deficit is that it promotes change and a new way of looking at things. There are many Americans who would like to start their own business. Now may be the perfect time to start up one. It is never too late or too early for someone to start thinking about opening up a local business, even if it is out of his or her home. Opening up a local business builds up the workforce within the United States and creates more opportunities for the exporting of products and services.

The U.S. Trade Representative held a conference in January 2010 with the intent to boost homegrown jobs and global exports for small and medium-sized businesses. The nation's lead trade policy agency, which is connected with small and medium-sized businesses across the United States, met at a conference event titled "Jobs on Main Street, Customers Around the World: A Positive Trade Agenda for

The U.S. Trade Representative Ron Kirk works for the American people by helping medium- and smaller-sized businesses find ways to increase their exports, which in turn will help decrease the trade deficit.

U.S. Small and Medium-Sized Enterprises." The event was part of a weeklong effort to support the recovery of the U.S. economy by increasing the amount of exports. The U.S. Trade Representative is aiming to make trade policy work better for America's small and medium-sized businesses because they are the country's biggest job creators and have a lot of export possibilities. The way the job market is now, with so many people competing for so few jobs, there is a great need to grow jobs domestically.

If America starts to expand more of its exports into foreign markets, as opposed to depending so much on imports, it will provide these small and medium-sized businesses the opportunity to grow. When businesses grow and demand becomes higher for their products, these businesses can increase their workforce and create more jobs. That way, they are competing on a global level, but the jobs stay here in the United States instead of being sent to other countries. This is a strategy that will not happen overnight, so it is important for American teenagers to start thinking about what type of field they want to get into. If someone is interested in starting a business, it is a good idea to work on a business plan and talk to someone who owns a similar local business.

Tim Herbert, who works with CompTIA, an information technology trade association, presented a study where small and medium-sized businesses gave their impressions of trade barriers and opportunities. Eighty-six percent of the businesses in the study stated that their export sales were growing faster than sales within the United States. As the barriers for trade break down, it will be easier for "Main Street" businesses in America to sell their goods and services around the world. This will ultimately lead to well-paying jobs for American citizens.

The National Export Initiative

The National Export Initiative was introduced by President Barack Obama in his State of the Union address on January 27, 2010. The two major goals of this initiative are:

- Double the amount the United States exports over the next five years.
- Add two million jobs in America.
- According to the initiative, American small and medium-sized businesses that want to export will have strong support from the U.S. government. The three main issues that will be focused on are:

  o Expanding the U.S. government's efforts to promote exports especially for small and medium-sized businesses by encouraging these businesses to export internationally.
  o Improving access to credit, especially for small and medium-sized businesses that want to export.
  o Increasing the government's focus on knocking down barriers that prevent U.S. companies from getting open and fair access to foreign markets.

THE CURRENT VALUE OF THE U.S. DOLLAR

When the value of the U.S. dollar decreases, the goods that are produced in America become cheaper. When prices of American goods drop, they become more competitive when compared to goods produced by foreign countries. Also, because the value is less, it increases U.S. exports because the prices of the goods are more appealing. This will help boost economic growth but also lead to the price of petroleum increasing. Whenever the American dollar decreases, the price of oil is raised in order for profit margins to be maintained in countries selling to the United States. There is more money leaving the United States to buy the same amount of oil that it is used to purchasing.

According to the *New York Times*, the demand for American products abroad is starting to recover with the help of the weak dollar. As of September, the trade deficit was running at an annual rate of $366 billion, about half of the $695.9 billion last year. The deficit with China, which had been lessening, rose 9.2 percent to $22.1 billion last month, its highest level in ten months. While the economy remains weak, Nariman Behravesh, chief economist at IHS Global Insight in Lexington, Massachusetts, says, "The rise in imports might indicate that manufacturers in the United States were building inventories—a carmaker importing Japanese auto parts, for instance—in anticipation of higher demand from American consumers. It's a very strong signal that the domestic economy is recovering."

Whenever there is news that imports and exports are rising, it indicates that there is economic growth. This is the positive news that the United States needs to boost its economy. This will ensure a strong job market and higher standard of living as teens get ready to enter the workforce.

CHAPTER SIX
MAKING A DIFFERENCE

Economic phenomena such as the trade deficit bring about changes in the economy of a nation. When a country is faced with a crisis such as high unemployment rates, creativity and ingenuity come out. Unemployment takes people out of their comfort zones and forces them to try things that they would not have otherwise, such as opening up their own business or finding savvy ways to reduce spending and oil consumption. There are many ways that young adults can become part of this positive change to turn the trade deficit around. It is never too early or too late to think of small business ideas or look into a trade skill that peaks your interest.

HIGH-DEMAND JOBS

According to John Stamos of Defender Capital, teenagers should turn off the television and take the time to learn non-exportable jobs like plumbing, electrical work, or a high-tech job so that they can compete in the twenty-first century. These are service-type jobs that are needed and support the U.S. economy. Apprenticeships are also another great way to learn a trade that is in high demand. Some apprenticeships even pay for you to go to school. The U.S. Department of Labor is a great place to research what types of jobs are in demand, as well as career voyages.

Structured on-the-job training is often given in high-demand jobs, such as positions in the field of technology.

According to the U.S. Department of Labor, "Registered Apprenticeship programs meet the skilled workforce needs of American industry, training millions of qualified individuals for lifelong careers since 1937." Registered Apprenticeships help mobilize the American workforce by providing structured, on-the-job learning in industries such as construction and manufacturing. They also provide training in industries such as health care, information technology, energy, telecommunications, and more. The Registered Apprenticeship program offers an individual an open door to about one thousand career areas, including the following top occupations:

- Able seaman
- Carpenter
- Chef
- Child care development specialist
- Construction craft laborer
- Dental assistant
- Electrician
- Elevator constructor
- Fire medic
- Law enforcement agent

- Truck driver
- Pipefitter

Talking with a career counselor at school is also a great way to figure out what types of jobs one might be interested in. It is never too early to think about what you want to do in life. Asking questions and doing research will ensure that you choose a career path that is right for you and the betterment of the community that you live in.

Decreasing Dependency on Oil

Here are five simple ways to decrease our dependency on oil:

- **When going to school, carpool with friends, ride your bike, walk, or take mass transit. This will decrease the amount of gas that you use.**
- **If you are looking into getting a car, purchase one that is fuel-efficient.**
- **Encourage your parents and school administrators to turn down the thermostat by two degrees, which will cut back on the amount of gas used to heat the house and school.**
- **Instead of using plastic bags when shopping, bring your own reusable cloth bags or ask for paper bags that can be recycled. All plastics are largely a petroleum by-product.**
- **Air-dry your clothes instead of using a dryer. Even though your dryer is electric, it takes gas to produce the electricity.**

RECYCLE

Recyclable materials are bought and sold just like any other product. Recycling American goods means using domestically produced material for production and then selling American-made goods. People who prefer to buy recyclable goods instead of similar foreign-made goods help reduce the trade deficit.

Find creative ways to reduce, reuse, or recycle. There are hundreds of Web sites, blogs, books, and magazines that teach and give ideas on how to reuse and remake what is already at home. When a person recycles, there are numerous financial, environmental, and social returns. According to the U.S. Environmental Protection Agency (EPA), there are several benefits to recycling. They include:

- Protecting and expanding U.S. manufacturing jobs and increasing U.S. competitiveness.
- Reducing the need for land filling and incineration.
- Preventing pollution caused by the manufacturing of products from virgin materials.
- Saving energy (reducing the need for oil).
- Decreasing emissions of greenhouse gases that contribute to global climate change.
- Conserving natural resources such as timber, water, and minerals.
- Helping sustain the environment for future generations.

If Americans are recycling and then selling those materials, the money comes back to American pockets, whether it is sold in the United States or another country. When shopping at a big-box store or the local grocery store, notice that more of today's products such as sponges, shoes, and tile are being constructed with partial—if not total—recycled material. There are also many new innovative applications that people have come up with for recycled material, such as recovered glass used in roadway asphalt, recovered plastic in carpeting, and paper to make countertops.

As demand grows in the United States for more environmentally sustainable products, manufacturers will want to meet that demand. If this can be encouraged, more jobs will be created in this area for future generations. This will give the United States more products to export as long as the manufacturing portion is kept within the borders of the country. So not only is a person helping the trade deficit, but he or she is also helping the environment.

DECREASE DEPENDENCY ON PETROLEUM PRODUCTS

One of the biggest things pushing up the trade deficit is American dependency on petroleum imports. According to FuelEconomy. gov, "Over half of the oil we use is imported (57 percent), and our dependence will increase as we use up domestic resources." The oil reserves that most of the world imports are concentrated

Americans can buy recycled products, even when shopping at big-box stores. Recycled alternatives reduce the trade deficit by saving American jobs, energy, and the environment.

in the Middle East. According to the U.S. Department of Energy, Congress recently passed legislation "to decrease our dependence on oil by increasing corporate average fuel economy (CAFE) standards on new cars and trucks to 35 mpg by

Think of ways to decrease oil dependency in transportation. Take forms of mass transit, such as buses or trains. Small changes in the way a person travels can make a big difference.

model year 2020. This could reduce our petroleum use by 25 billion gallons by 2030."

In December 2009, the U.S. deficit widened by more than what was expected. This occurred because the United States imported more oil products at higher prices. When oil prices increase, companies have to increase the price of their products. They increase those prices because they are paying more for the product to be made and transported to their stores. They do this so that they can cover all of these costs and still make as much money as they were before.

EDUCATE YOURSELF AND BECOME INVOLVED

Some of the best ways to create change are by educating oneself, becoming involved, and sharing your knowledge with those around you. Be creative and find ways to live simply. Think about every purchase made and whether or not it is a necessity to have the latest and greatest iPod or cell phone. Find ways to repurpose an article of clothing or a bike instead of going out and buying a brand new one. You will be supporting a local business and the American economy.

Americans are overconsumers and need to start making better choices when it comes to how they spend their money.

Choosing to alter one's lifestyle in small ways makes a difference when it comes to the trade deficit. Biking is an inexpensive way to travel. It also decreases oil consumption.

The simpler one's life is, the less stressful life becomes. Material things fade with time. People outgrow clothes and fashions fade, but the relationships you have with those around you can make an impression that lasts forever.

The trade deficit in this country is a result of overspending on cheap products and services. If every teenager does his or her part to reverse this trend, others will see it and it will have a positive effect on many areas of life. Take the time to learn where the products being purchased come from and find out how the local economy can be supported.

Ten Great Questions
to Ask an Economist

1 How does the trade deficit affect me?

2 What can I do to help reduce the trade deficit?

3 How does the trade deficit affect our national security?

4 How bad is our trade deficit compared to other countries?

5 Is a trade deficit necessarily bad for our economy?

6 How does globalization affect our trade deficit?

7 What countries are our strongest competitors for global trade?

8 How do we prevent future trade deficits?

9 Is globalization good for our economy?

10 Will the trade deficit directly influence my chances for future employment?

GLOSSARY

capital flow When money for investment moves from one country to another.

consumer Someone who buys goods or services for his or her own personal, family, household, or other non-business use.

domestic Something that is from or in one's own country.

economic growth An increase in a nation's ability to produce goods and services.

free trade Trade between countries without the barriers of protective customs tariffs.

globalization The increased flow of goods, services, money, and ideas beyond national borders.

interdependence When people or businesses depend on or help each other.

low wage A low payment for labor or services to a worker on an hourly, daily, or weekly basis or by the piece.

manufacture To take a raw material and make it into a finished product, especially by means of a large-scale industrial operation.

multilateral trade Trade between many nations at one time.

multinational corporation A company that has operations in more than one nation.

nontariff barrier Government measures other than tariffs that restrict imports or have the potential for restricting international trade.

Office of the U.S. Trade Representative The executive agency that administers the president's policies on international trade.

profit margin The amount of profit made from selling a product.

secretary of commerce Secretary of the federal department that promotes and administers domestic and foreign trade.

standard of living The level of material comfort in terms of goods and services that are available to people.

tariff A tax imposed on imports by a government.

trade association Individuals and companies in a specific business or industry organized to promote common interests.

trade balance A balance between the exporting and importing of goods and services.

trade deficit When there are more imports coming into a country than what is exported.

value How much something is worth.

FOR MORE INFORMATION

International Trade Administration
U.S. Department of Commerce
1401 Constitution Avenue NW
Washington, DC 20230
(800) USA-TRAD(E) [872-8723]
Web site: http://www.trade.gov
The mission of this government agency is to create pros-
    perity by strengthening the competitiveness of U.S.
    industry, promoting trade and investment, and
    ensuring fair trade and compliance with trade laws
    and agreements.

Office of the U.S. Trade Representative
600 17th Street NW
Washington, DC 20508
Web site: http://www.ustr.gov
The Office of the U.S. Trade Representative is responsible
    for developing and coordinating U.S. international trade,
    commodity, and direct investment policy and overseeing
    negotiations with other countries.

Statistics Canada
150 Tunney's Pasture Driveway

Ottawa, ON K1A 0T6
Canada
(800) 263-1136
Web site: http://www.statcan.gc.ca/start-debut-eng.html
Statistics Canada produces statistics that help Canadians
    better understand their country's population, resources,
    economy, society, and culture. It is legislated to serve
    this function for the whole of Canada and each of the
    provinces.

U.S. Census Bureau on Foreign Trade
4600 Silver Hill Road
Washington, DC 20233
301-763-INFO (4636) or 800-923-8282
Web site: http://www.census.gov/foreign-trade/index.html
The U.S. Census Bureau on Foreign Trade is the official
    source for U.S. export and import statistics, information
    on export regulations, commodity classifications, and other
    trade-related topics.

U.S. Department of Commerce
1401 Constitution Avenue NW
Washington, DC 20230
(202) 482-2000
Web site: http://www.commerce.gov
This department has a broad mandate to advance economic
    growth and opportunities for Americans. It has cross-
    cutting responsibilities in the areas of trade, technology,
    entrepreneurship, economic development, environmental
    stewardship, and statistical research and analysis.

World Trade Organization
Centre William Rappard
Rue de Lausanne 154, CH-1211
Geneva 21, Switzerland
Web site: http://www.wto.org
The World Trade Organization provides a place for
negotiating agreements that are directed at reducing bar-
riers to international trade and making sure that there is a
level playing field for all who are a part of the organization.

WEB SITES

Due to the changing nature of Internet links, Rosen Publishing
has developed an online list of Web sites related to the subject
of this book. This site is updated regularly. Please use this link
to access the list:

http://www.rosenlinks.com/rwe/htdw

FOR FURTHER READING

Andrews, David. *Business Without Borders*. Portsmouth, NH: Heinemann Educational Books, 2010.

Cooper, Adriam. *Fair Trade?: A Look at the Way the World is Today* (Issues of the World). Mankato, MN: Stargazer Books, 2005.

Lee, Sally. *Sam Walton: Business Genius of Wal-Mart* (People to Know Today). Berkeley Heights, NJ: Enslow Publishers, 2007.

Miller, Debra. *Fair Trade* (Current Controversies). Farmington Hills, MI: Greenhaven Press, 2010.

Miller, Debra. *Importing from China* (Current Controversies). Farmington Hills, MI: Greenhaven Press, 2009.

Reiss, Ronald. *The World Trade Organization* (Global Organizations). New York, NY: Chelsea House Publications, 2009.

Swartz, Jon. *Young Wealth: Trade Secrets from Teens Who Are Changing American Business*. Bloomington, Indiana: Rooftop Publishing, 2006.

Young, Michelle. *Free Trade* (Opposing Viewpoints). Farmington Hills, MI: Greenhaven Press, 2008.

BIBLIOGRAPHY

Bernstein, William. *A Splendid Exchange: How Trade Shaped the World*. New York, NY: Atlantic Monthly Press, 2008.

Destler, I. M. *American Trade Politics*. Washington, DC: Institute for International Economics, 2005.

Dicken, Peter. *Global Shift: Transforming the World Economy*. New York, NY: The Guilford Press, 1998.

The Economist. "Oil and the Current Account." 2010. Retrieved January 13, 2010 (http://www.economist.com/blogs/freeexchange/2010/02/americas_trade_deficit).

Frontline World. "The North American Free Trade Agreement (NAFTA) and the Mexican Economy." Retrieved January 39, 2010 (http://www.pbs.org/frontlineworld/stories/mexico403/links.html#03).

Global Policy Forum. "Globalization (General Analysis on Globalization)." Retrieved February 18, 2010 (http://www.globalpolicy.org/globalization.html).

Healy, Jack. "U.S. Regional Economies Slip and Trade Deficit Grows" 2009. Retrieved January 13, 2010 (http://www.nytimes.com/2009/06/11/business/economy/11econ.html).

Hughes, Sandra. "Consumer Revolt Against Lead Toys." Retrieved January 21, 2010 (http://www.cbsnews.com/stories/2009/12/04/eveningnews/main5894047.shtml).

Miller, Debra. *Importing from China*. Farmington Hills, MI: Greenhaven Press, 2009.

Office of the U.S. Trade Representative. "President Obama Lays Out Export Initiative to Create Jobs." 2010. Retrieved January 28, 2010 (http://www.ustr.gov/about-us/press-office/blog/2010/january/president-obama-lays-out-export-initiative-create-jobs).

Office of the U.S. Trade Representative. "U.S. Trade Representative Seeks to Boost Home-Grown Jobs, Global Exports for America's Small- and Medium-Sized Businesses." 2010. Retrieved January 28, 2010 (http://www.ustr.gov/about-us/press-office/blog/2010/january/us-trade-representative-seeks-boost-home-grown-jobs-global-e).

Ojha, Shruti. "The Economic and Legal Analysis of Dumping." 2008. Retrieved January 28, 2010 (http://www.globalpolitician.com/23989-business).

Persky, Joseph, and Wim Wiewel. *When Corporations Leave Town*. Detroit, MI: Wayne State University Press, 2000.

Schlisserman, Courtney. "Trade Deficit in U.S. Unexpectedly Widened on Imports." 2010. Retrieved January 28, 2010 (http://www.businessweek.com/news/2010-02-10/trade-deficit-in-u-s-probably-narrowed-as-exports-increased.html).

U.S. Census Foreign Trade Statistics. "U.S. International Trade in Goods and Services Highlights." 2010. Retrieved January 21, 2010 (http://www.census.gov/indicator/www/ustrade.html).

U.S. Department of Labor. "Minimum Wage." Retrieved January 13, 2010 (http://www.dol.gov/dol/topic/wages/minimumwage.htm).

U.S. Environmental Protection Agency. "Recycling."
   Retrieved January 22, 2010 (http://www.epa.gov/
   osw/conserve/rrr/recycle.htm).

U.S. Trade Deficit Review Commission. *The U.S.
   Trade Deficit: Causes. Consequences and
   Recommendations for Action*. U.S. Trade Deficit Review
   Commission, 2000.

Wells, Jane. "China's "Dumping" Leaves U.S. Hanging . . .
   Its Clothes." 2008. Retrieved January 28, 2010 (http://
   www.cnbc.com/id/23845462).

INDEX

About the Author

Kate Canino is an author and educator living in Rochester, New York. A graduate of the College of Saint Rose in childhood education, she is always trying to inspire kids to find ways to recycle and repurpose things in their homes and not feel the need to consume so much stuff. The economy has always been a topic of conversation in her home, as her father and two brothers work in the field of finance.

Photo Credits

Cover (top) © www.istockphoto.com/Lilli Day; cover (bottom), pp. 1 (right), 41 Jim R. Bounds/Bloomberg via Getty Images; pp. 1 (left), 3, 4–5 © www.istockphoto.com/Dean Turner; pp. 6–7 Patrick Hertzog/AFP/Getty; pp. 8, 18, 29, 40, 49, 57 Mario Tama/Getty Images; pp. 9, 64–65 Joe Raedle/Getty Images; pp. 10–11 David McNew/Getty Images; pp. 12–13 Adam Dean/Bloomberg via Getty Images; pp. 20–21 Dirck Halstead/Time-Life Pictures/Getty Images; pp. 22–23 Fabrice Coffrini/AFP/Getty Images; pp. 24–25, 47 © AP Images; pp. 30–31 Bobby Bank/Getty Images; pp. 32–33 Mario Tama/Getty Images; pp. 36–37 John Giustina/Iconica/Getty Images; p. 38 Smiley N. Pool-Pool/Getty Images; p. 45 Spencer Platt/Getty Images; pp. 50–51 Tim Sloan-Pool/Getty Images; p. 53 Tim Sloan/AFP/Getty Images; pp. 58–59 Jason Janik/Bloomberg via Getty Images; pp. 62–63 Daniel Acker/Bloomberg via Getty Images; pp. 66–67 Smith Collection/Iconica/Getty Images; pp. 69, 71, 74–75, 78 © www.istockphoto.com/studiovision.

Editor: Nicholas Croce; Photo Researcher: Marty Levick